TIME TRAVELING TO
1983

CELEBRATING A SPECIAL YEAR

TIME TRAVELING TO 1983

Author
Michael B. Allen

Design
Gonçalo Sousa

December 2022
ISBN: 9798367220841

Surprise!

Dear reader, thank you so much for purchasing my book!

To make this book more (much more!) affordable, the images are all black & white, but I've created a special gift for you!

You can now have access, for FREE, to the PDF version of this book with the original images!

Keep in mind that some are originally black & white, but a lot of them are colored.

Go to page 101 and follow the instructions to download it.

I hope you enjoy it!

Contents

Chapter I: News & Current Events 1983

Leading Events

January 19th: Nazi War Criminal Klaus Barbie Arrested

Klaus Barbie

During World War II, German SS and SD operative Nikolaus 'Klaus' Barbie worked in Vichy France and was given the nickname 'Butcher of Lyon' because he tortured prisoners while he was the head of the Gestapo in Lyon, France. When the war ended, he worked for the United States intelligence services because of his efforts against communism, and they helped him escape to Bolivia.

In 1983 he was extradited to France to face 41 counts of crimes against humanity, based on the depositions of 730 Jews and French Resistance survivors. They each described how Barbie tortured and murdered the prisoners.

He was subsequently convicted and sentenced to life in prison. In 1991, Barbie died of leukemia while serving his life sentence at a prison in Lyon.

January 31st: UK Passes Seatbelt Law

A new law came into force in the UK on January 31st, 1983, where all drivers and front-seat passengers were required to wear seatbelts. It came after 15 years of debate surrounding the law, and it had previously been attempted to bring into law 11 times. The Conservative Government and the Labour Official Opposition were against the law, but consistent campaigning by safety organizations and medical groups finally won in the end.

Following the introduction of the new law, it was observed that 90% of drivers and front seat passengers were wearing their seatbelts. The new law also saw a reduction of fatalities by 29% and a 30% decrease in serious injuries that year.

Echo Reporter Gill Dawson is pictured fastening her seatbelt ahead of the new law

February 18th: The Nellie Massacre

Victims of Assam's Nellie Massacre

The Nellie Massacre occurred for six hours on the morning of February 18th, 1983, in Assam, India. During the massacre, 2,191 people, predominantly Muslims, were killed. Native rural peasants rampaged across fourteen villages in Assam, killing Muslims. It is believed the violence was a result of the controversial state elections during the Assam Agitation after Indira Gandhi allowed 4 million Bangladesh immigrants to vote.

The official report on the massacre, which was 600 pages long, has largely been kept a secret, and only three copies of the report exist. The Assam Government 1984 and the Congress Government, along with subsequent governments, decided to keep it from the public.

Following the massacre, Police filed a total of 688 criminal cases. Of these, 378 were closed because of a lack of evidence. Eventually, in 1985, the remainder of the cases were dropped by the Government of India. To date, nobody has been charged with any crimes associated with the massacre.

Other Major Events

September 17th: Vanessa Williams Crowned Miss America

On September 17th, 1983, Vanessa Williams made history as the first African American to win the crown of Miss America. At just 20 years of age, she endured a lot of criticism during her reign as Miss America due to her coloring, not just because she was black, but because she was light-skinned, and her eyes were not the typical brown of an African American. She even received death threats and hate mail.

Vanessa Williams Crowned Miss America

Two months before her reign was over, in July 1984, nude photos of Vanessa taken before she entered the Miss America pageant were published in Penthouse magazine without her consent. Vanessa believed the photographs had been destroyed, and she had never signed a release for them to be published. Because of the scandal, she was stripped of her crown.

On September 13th, 2015, 32 years after the scandal, Vanessa became a judge for Miss America. By now, she was a well-known singer and actress, and she performed a song during the pageant. Following her performance, the CEO of Miss America, Sam Haskell, issued a public apology to Vanessa for how she was treated during her reign as Miss America.

December 4th: US Navy Aviator Lt's. Mark Lange and Bobby Goodman Shot Down Over Lebanon

Bobby Goodman shortly after his release

During a bombing mission over Lebanon on December 4th, 1983, the aircraft flown by Lt. Lange and Goodman was struck by a missile. With the aircraft on fire, and the eruption of one of the engines, Lt. Lange desperately tried to gain control of the aircraft so the crew could eject, but the aircraft stalled and subsequently crashed on a hill. Both Lange and Goodman were ejected in the final moments before the crash, but Lange's parachute didn't deploy correctly, and on hitting the ground, his leg was injured severely. Troops from Syria and Lebanese civilians captured both men, and Lange died soon after from his injuries. Goodman also suffered injuries, including shoulder and knee injuries and three broken ribs. His captors transported him to Damascus.

Over the next month, while Goodman was held captive, the United States government made multiple attempts to have him freed. In January 1984, Reverend Jesse Jackson made the journey to Syria and Libya along with a group of 20 volunteers. They were able to secure the release of Goodman peacefully. A few days after his release, on January 4th, 1984, Lt. Goodman was welcomed to the White House by President Ronald Reagan.

December 10th: Nobel Prize in Literature Awarded to William Golding

William Golding received the Nobel Prize in Literature on December 10th, 1983, for the novels he had written, most notably, the Lord of the Flies. This book was later adapted for a play and a film and was widely read in schools all over the world.

Golding published a further 12 novels during his lifetime, and in 1980 he received the Booker Prize for one of his sea trilogy novels, the Rites of Passage. He was knighted in 1988 because of his contributions to literature and was ranked third in The Time's '50 Greatest British Writers Since 1945'.

William Golding receiving the Nobel Prize in Literature

Political Events

February 12th: 100 Women Protest in Lahore, Pakistan

A protest march led by the Women's Action Forum and the Punjab Women Lawyers Association took place on February 12th, 1983, in Lahore, Pakistan. They were protesting against the Law of Evidence and other Hudood Ordinances, which were discriminatory towards women. The Law of Evidence would reduce the value of women's testimony to half the value of a man's testimony. As they marched, Police used tear gas and batons against the women, and many were injured. At least 50 of the women marching were arrested for defying the law against public assembly. This march was groundbreaking in that women had very little rights at the time and seldom spoke up for fear of retaliation, but on this one day, they all came together to protest.

Zhila Shah being baton charged by the police

Despite all of this, the women were eventually successful in repealing the Law of Evidence. Since 2012, the official commemoration of the protest has been held called Pakistan's National Women's Day.

February 24th: Congress of the United States Releases Report Regarding Japanese Internment During World War II

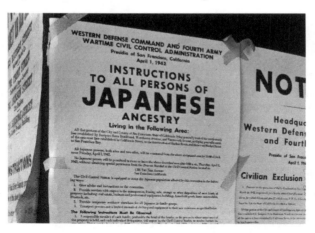

Posters ordered Japanese American citizens to report for internment

Throughout World War II, the United States incarcerated and relocated around 120,000 people of Japanese ancestry who resided on the Pacific Coast to camps in the western part of the country. It is estimated that two-thirds of the people incarcerated were actually American citizens.

President Franklin D. Roosevelt made the executive order to incarcerate people of Japanese descent following the attack on Pearl Harbor by Japan.

In California, if a person had 1/16th or more of Japanese ancestry, they were eligible for incarceration.

Japanese Internment Camps

In the 1970s, President Jimmy Carter, under pressure from the Japanese American Citizens League, opened an investigation into the incarceration of Japanese Americans during World War II to determine if the government had been justified in its decision. The Commission of Wartime Relocation and Interment of Civilians was formed to investigate. The Commission's report was released in 1983 and was aptly named the Personal Justice Denied report. It found that there had been minimal disloyalty by the Japanese at the time, and in conclusion, the incarceration had been racist. The report recommended reparation be paid to those who had been incarcerated at the camps.

President Ronald Reagan signs the Civil Liberties Act of 1988

The Civil Liberties Act of 1988 was signed by President Ronald Reagan, which was an official apology on behalf of the government and a payment of $20,000 was to be paid to each person who had been incarcerated that was still alive at the time the Act was signed. By 1992, $1.6 billion had been paid in reparations.

June 9th: Margaret Thatcher Wins by Landslide in General Election in the UK

Margaret Thatcher

The UK general election was held on June 9th, 1983. Despite having a difficult first term as Prime Minister, Margaret Thatcher, the leader of the Conservative Party, won the election by the most decisive victory since 1945, with a 144-seat majority. The turnaround by the public towards the Conservative Party was partly due to the success of the Falklands War and the ensuing growth of the economy. Margaret Thatcher, often referred to as the 'Iron Lady' because of her strength and will, was Prime Minister of the United Kingdom from 1979 – 1990 and is often considered to be one of the most impactful leaders of modern times.

Other Notable Events

January 26th: Red Rain in the UK

A weather phenomenon often called blood rain struck the UK on January 26th, 1983. While seemingly disturbing to many people, this fairly rare red rain is not sinister at all, and in fact, there is a logical explanation for it occurring. Red rain, or blood rain, occurs when winds in the Sahara Desert send sand into the atmosphere, which is then returned to Earth in raindrops. The sand of the Sahara has a red hue, so when it mixes with the raindrops, it gives the appearance that blood is falling from the sky. There have been cases of red rain for centuries,

Southampton marathon in the red rain

and it was once believed to be actual blood falling from the sky. In earlier centuries, it was blamed on the occult and was considered to be an evil omen when it occurred.

Other theories behind the phenomenon include the presence of specific micro-organisms in the raindrops or sunspots, but the general consensus in the scientific community is that it is indeed from the sands of the Sahara Desert.

February 2nd: Giovanni Vigliotto Charged with Polygamy Involving 105 Women

Giovanni Vigliotto during his trial

The trial for bigamy and fraud of Giovanni Vigliotto began on February 2nd, 1983. Vigliotto claimed to have married 105 women all over the globe and would swindle them out of their money and possessions before moving on to the next unsuspecting lady. The trial case was regarding his marriage to real estate agent Patricia Ann Gardiner, who it was claimed Vigliotto had swindled out of $36,500 in November 1981.

Vigliotto claimed his real name was Nikolai Peruskov, but it was later contended that his real name was Fred Jipp. During the trial, he produced a list of 50 aliases he had used and the list of wives and their addresses, and the dates when he married each of them. He offered to plead guilty to bigamy if the fraud charges were dropped, but the prosecution refused. Among his wild claims, Vigliotto stated he had worked for the Central Intelligence Agency from 1953-1954, which further enabled him to travel around the world, meeting women and marrying them under his various aliases.

The jury took just 24 minutes to deliberate the charges, after which they found him guilty. He was sentenced to 34 years in prison.

February 8th: Racehorse Shergar is Kidnapped and Held for Ransom

One of the most famous thoroughbred racehorses of all time was a horse called Shergar. On February 8th, 1983, groom Jim Fitzgerald answered a knock at his door and was faced with two gunmen wearing masks. They forced Fitzgerald to take them to the stable where Shergar was located, and six more armed men appeared. Shergar was put into a horsebox, and Fitzgerald was forced into the car along with the armed men.

Three hours later, Fitzgerald was allowed to escape. They wanted $3 million in return for the horse. It was decided that the ransom would not be paid. Shergar was never seen alive again.

Although never proven, it was suspected that

Shergar, ridden by Walter Swinburn

the Irish Republican Army (IRA) was behind the kidnapping. An IRA informant, Sean O'Callaghan, claimed the horse was killed within the first 24 hours of the kidnapping. He claimed that the horse had broken one of his legs during the transportation, and so they shot him with a machine gun to put him out of his misery.

In 1999, an annual race held at the Ascot Racecourse in the UK was named the Shergar Cup in remembrance of the famous horse.

April 8th: Magician Makes the Statue of Liberty Disappear

One of the most spectacular magical illusions to ever occur took place on April 8th, 1983, when David Copperfield made the Statue of Liberty disappear in front of a

David Copperfield, the magician who made the Statue of Liberty disappear

live audience. While a well-known magician at the time, this event shot Copperfield to a whole new level of stardom as the televised trick went around the world.

Copperfield stood in front of the audience, and two large pillars with a screen between them stood in front of the Statue of Liberty. When the screen went up and came back down, the Statue had disappeared. Then when the screen went up and came back down again, the Statue reappeared. An enormous feat when considering how big the Statue of liberty is. But it was later revealed how he was able to conduct the trick. The live audience was seated on a platform, and Copperfield distracted them with loud music, so they didn't notice that the platform they were seated on was actually moving.

By shifting the position of the platform, the perspective was changed, and the Statue was actually hidden by one of the big pillars holding the screen. The lighting on the pillars was so bright that it was impossible to see the Statue behind them.

June 18th: First American Woman Launched into Space

Sally Ride was the first American woman to go into space, which drew an immense amount of media attention. She received a staggering 500 requests for interviews, and she declined every one of them.

Launch of STS-7, 1st US Woman in Space

NASA hosted a press conference like they normally did before a launch, on May 24th, 1983, and some of the questions she was asked were a bit bizarre. She was asked if her reproductive organs would be affected and if she cried when things went wrong. The NASA engineers even asked Ride to help them create a makeup kit for space because they presumed that as a woman, this would be important to her. They even offered to supply her with 100 tampons – it was a six-day trip!

The crew of the STS-7

Not only was Ride the first American female to launch into space, but she was also only the third woman ever in the world. At the launch, many spectators were spotted in T-shirts saying 'Ride, Sally Ride,' which were from the lyrics of the song 'Mustang Sally' by Wilson Pickett.

Ride became somewhat of a celebrity, and after she returned to Earth, she spent a few months on tour visiting the Governor of California, the Mayor of New York, and the Congressional Space Caucus. She was asked to appear with Bob Hope, but she thought he was a sexist, so she declined.

July 21st: Lowest Temperature Recorded in Antarctica

The Russian Vostok research station located in Antarctica recorded the lowest temperature on Earth on July 21st, 1983. It was during the winter of the southern hemisphere, and the temperature recorded was -89.2°C or -128.6°F. This was 54 degrees colder than the

Recorded at Vostok Station, altitude 3489m on the polar plateau

average temperature in winter in Antarctica.

There was a flow of cold air circling around the station, and this prevented the warmer air from the Southern Ocean from entering the area. Also, there was 'diamond dust' in the air, which is where tiny ice particles are suspended in the air, which also contributed to the plummet in temperature.

September 2nd: Cyclosporine is Approved by the FDA

The drug cyclosporine was approved by the Food and Drug Administration in America on September 2nd 1983. Cyclosporine can prevent or at least slow the rejection of transplanted organs by suppressing the immune system of the body. Rejection is the largest cause of death in transplant patients, so its usage revolutionized organ transplantation.

The food and drug commissioner, Arthur Hull Hayes Jr., approved the drug on his last day of work, after processing 123 volumes of data in nine months, whereas it normally took at least two years to approve a new drug.

Cyclosporine

During clinical trials, cyclosporine doubled the success rate of liver and kidney transplants. It is also used in other diseases such as chronic hives, severe atopic dermatitis, pyoderma gangrenosum, Kimura disease, and many others. It is often useful in patients who don't respond to steroid treatments.

October 4th: Richard Noble Sets New Land Speed Record

Richard Noble

British driver and entrepreneur Richard Noble set a new land speed record at the Black Rock Desert in Nevada on October 4th, 1983. Driving his vehicle Thrust2, he reached an average speed of 633mph, or more than 1000kph. The record he broke had been long-standing for 13 years and was held by Gary Gabelich in The Blue Flame vehicle.

The speed was recorded across 12 miles (20km) of a dried flat lakebed in Black Rock. Each run consisted of an approximate distance of 10.5 miles, and the time it took to cover the distance was 110 seconds. The fastest single run the Thrust 2 made was 650.88mph (1047.490 kph). Later that year, Noble was awarded an Officer of the Empire honor.

The Thrust2 was a jet-propelled car designed and built in Britain. It was powered by a single jet engine from Rolls Royce. Thrust2 is 8,331 mm (328.0 in) long and 2,540 mm (100 in) wide and 2,134 mm (84.0 in) high including the tail fins. The vehicle alone has a height of 1.30 m (4 ft 3 in). The wheelbase is 6.35 m (20.8 ft), the front axle track is 2,007 mm (79.0 in), and that of the rear axle is 2,464 mm (97.0 in). The turning circle of Thrust2 is 45.7 m (150 ft).

The car that Richard Noble drove in 1983

The vehicle has a ground clearance of 127 mm (5.0 in). The two fuel tanks can hold a maximum of 563.7 l (124.0 imp gal; 148.9 US gal) of 'Jet A 1' kerosene fuel. The total weight is 3,900 kg (8,600 lb.).

Thrust2 is designed with two seats with a second cabin on the left side of the vehicle, so paying passengers or sponsors could be offered a 'ride-along' opportunity up to 200 mph.

September 23rd: Kentucky Fried Chicken Murders

Romeo Pinkerton and Darnell Hartsfield

On the night of September 23rd, 1983, armed robbers entered the Kentucky Fried Chicken restaurant in Kilgore, Texas, just before it closed. There were five people in the restaurant at the time, some who were staff and others who were waiting for a staff member to finish work for the night. All five people were kidnapped and taken to a field on County Road 232. There, they were all killed with a gunshot to the back of their head. One victim was located a little way away from the others, and she had been raped before she was executed. Local Police, along with Texas Rangers, discovered the bodies of Joey Johnson (20), David Maxwell (20), Mary Tyler (37), Monty Landers (19), and Opie Hughes (29).

The case was unsolved for 22 years, despite a number of people being arrested during that time. After the discovery of a piece of a fingernail on one of the victims, James Earl Mankins Jr. was arrested. The son of Jimmy Mankins, the state representative, James Earl Mankins Jr., had a history of drug offenses. He was charged with murder, but the case was dropped when DNA analysis determined it was not his fingernail.

Two men who were in prison for other offenses were charged in November 2005 for the murders. Romeo Pinkerton (47) and Darnell Hartsfield (44) were facing the death penalty if they were convicted of the murders.

On October 29th, 2007, Pinkerton pleaded guilty to five counts of murder and, as a plea deal, received five life sentences instead of the death penalty. Hartsfield was convicted in 2007 and also received a life sentence.

Investigators believed a third perpetrator was involved because of DNA found on the body of Opie Hughes, who had been raped. The DNA did not match Pinkerton nor Hartsfield, and they have never revealed who their accomplice had been.

September 25th: Maze Prison Mass Escape – Biggest Escape in British History

Maze Prison, located in County Antrim, Northern Ireland, was the scene of the biggest escape in British history on September 25th, 1983. The escape had been planned for months, and Gerry Kelly and Bobby Storey smuggled in handguns.

Some of the Maze escapees

They gained control by taking prison officers hostage. One officer was stabbed, and another officer was bashed in the head. Another officer who tried to stop the escape was shot in the head by Gerry Kelly but survived. A lorry arrived, and inmate Brendan McFarlane took the occupants hostage.

Twenty minutes later, the driver and a prison orderly went back to the lorry, and the driver's foot was tied to the clutch while 37 prisoners got into the lorry. Gerry Kelly lay on the floor of the cab with his gun pointing at the driver to ensure he did what he was told to do.

Officer James Ferris made a break for it and was stabbed in the chest by Dermot Finucane. Ferris collapsed and died before he could sound the alarm. Finucane stabbed the officer controlling the gate and two others who had just arrived. A soldier saw the incident and reported he had seen prison officers involved in a fight.

Prison officers used their cars to block the exit, so the prisoners made a run for the outer fence. By 4:18 pm, 35 prisoners had escaped the prison. They were meant to be greeted by 100 armed members of the IRA, but there was no transport there when they escaped. As a result of the escape, 20 prison officers were injured, with 13 beaten and kicked, two shot, and four stabbed.

November 4th: Serial Killer Dennis Nilsen Sentenced to Life Imprisonment

Dennis Nilsen

Scottish necrophile and serial killer Dennis Nilsen murdered 12 boys and young men at least between 1978 – 1983 in London. After they were killed, he would bathe the victim, dress them, and hold onto their bodies for a period of time before either cutting them up and flushing them down the toilet or burning them in a fire. After complaints about the plumbing, plumber Michael Cattran made a horrific discovery on February 8th, 1983. Cattran found the drain packed with what looked like flesh and small bones. He reported it to his supervisor, and they decided to go back and look the next morning. When they returned, the drain had been cleaned out, but they found some small pieces of bones and flesh in a pipe, and the Police were called. Nilsen was investigated and subsequently arrested.

Nilsen was found guilty of six counts of murder and two of attempted murder, and on November 4th, 1983, he was sentenced to life imprisonment without the possibility of parole. On May 12th, 2018, Nilsen died after undergoing surgical repair of an abdominal aortic aneurysm.

November 26th: Brink's-Mat Warehouse Robbery at Heathrow Airport

The Brink's-Mat warehouse, scene of the 1983 robbery

The Brink's-Mat warehouse, located at the Heathrow International Trading Estate at Heathrow Airport in London, was broken into by six robbers on November 26th, 1983. One of the robbers was a security guard at the warehouse, who enabled them to gain access. Inside the warehouse, they threatened the staff with a lit match after dousing them in petrol so they could get the combination number for the vault.

The robbers thought the vault was full of cash, but on entry, they discovered there were three tons of gold bullion along with diamonds and cash. The total they stole amounted to $37.5 million.

Two days later, witnesses saw a furnace being used in their neighbor's garden hut in Bath, Somerset, and notified the Police, thinking it may be linked to the robbery. The officers investigated but claimed it wasn't in their jurisdiction and they would notify the local Police in that area. However, it was not followed up on until 14 months later, when Police raided the property and found the furnace.

The occupier of the property, John Palmer, was a bullion dealer and jeweler, and he was arrested, though he claimed he did not know the gold was from the robbery, and the charges were dropped.

The security guard who had enabled the robbery to take place later gave the name of his brother-in-law, Brian Robinson, as one of the robbers, and Robinson was arrested in December 1983. The connection between Robinson and the guard was discovered, and the guard eventually confessed to his part in the robbery. Another of the robbers, Micky McAvoy, was arrested along with Kenneth Noye, who was trusted to dispose of the gold and was subsequently arrested. Noye was arrested after killing a police officer he found looking around his garden in January 1985.

McAvoy was sentenced to 25 years in prison, and the security guard received a sentence of 6 years. Noye was found guilty of conspiracy and received a 14-month sentence and a huge fine. He served seven years and was released in 1994. Later he committed another murder and was sentenced to life.

Chapter III: Entertainment 1983

Silver Screen

Top Film of 1983: Return of the Jedi

'Return of the Jedi,' the next installment of the 'Star Wars' franchise, was released on May 25th, 1983. Originally it was going to be released on May 27th, but it was changed to 2 days earlier because it was the same date that 'Star Wars' was released in 1977. The marketing campaign for 'Return of the Jedi' was massive and worldwide; initially, the teaser trailer stated the name of the movie was 'Revenge of the Jedi.' But George Lucas decided in December 1982 that the word 'Revenge' wasn't appropriate as a true Jedi should never seek revenge, and the original title

Return of the Jedi

was reinstated. By that time, thousands of posters with the name 'Revenge of the Jedi' were published and sent out, so they stopped shipping them out and sold the last 6,800 posters to fan club members for less than $10.

In the US and Canada, 'Return of the Jedi' grossed $309.3 million. The movie grossed $166 million in other countries, totaling $475.3 million worldwide. Not bad, considering the production budget was $32.5 million! On its opening weekend, encompassing 1,002 theaters, the film made $23 million, and in the first week, a record $45.3 million. For the first seven weeks it was released, the film finished in first place at the box office, except for the fourth weekend when it fell behind Superman III.

Remaining Top 3

Flashdance

Another top 10 film for 1983 was 'Flashdance,' which also had a booming soundtrack. The movie involved drama, romance, and dance and starred Jennifer Beals, who worked at a steel mill but dreamed of being a professional ballerina. It was the first time Jerry Bruckheimer and Don Simpson had produced together. Some more complex dance sequences were

Flashdance

filmed with a body double for Beals. Several hit songs were on the soundtrack, such as 'Maniac' by Michael Sembello and 'Flashdance…What a Feeling' sung by Irene Cara. The 'Flashdance… What a Feeling' song won the Academy Award for Best Original Song and a Golden Globe, among other awards. In May 1983, it reached number one on the 'Billboard Hot 100'. More than 700,000 copies of the soundtrack were sold within the first two weeks of its release, and to date has sold more than 6 million copies just in the United States.

Incidentally, the poster for the film had Beals wearing a sweatshirt with a really large hole at the neck, and many thought it was a cool fashion item but what had actually happened was that the sweatshirt shrunk in the wash, and she had to cut a large hole in it!

Octopussy

'Octopussy' was the 13th film in the James Bond series and the sixth of the series with Roger Moore in the lead role. The film's title came from a short story written by Ian Fleming, but the rest of the story was largely original. In 'Octopussy,' Bond follows a Soviet general (played by Steven Berkoff) stealing art and jewelry from the art repository at the Kremlin. Bond is led to exiled and wealthy Afghan prince Kamal Khan, played by Louis Jordan, and Octopussy, his associate, played by Maud Adams. They discover a plot to force Western Europe to disarm under the threat of a nuclear weapon. 'Octopussy' was released four months before the next franchise installment, 'Never Say Never Again.' With a budget of $27.5 million and mixed reviews, the film still earned $187.5 million.

Octopussy

Never Say Never Again

Unlike 'Octopussy,' 'Never Say Never Again' was produced by Taliafilm, not Eon Productions, which is why it was released so close to 'Octopussy.'

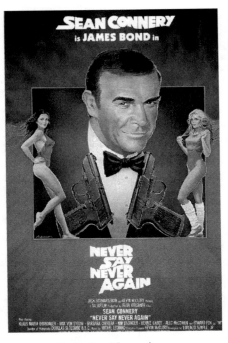

Never Say Never Again

This film was based on Ian Fleming's novel Thunderball. Kevin McClory, who had been one of the original writers of the Thunderball story, was the executive producer. For this film, Sean Connery played the lead role for what would be his seventh and last time as Bond. Because Connery was in his early 50s at the time of filming, the story featured an aging Bond who is brought back to investigate the theft by SPECTRE of nuclear weapons.

'Never Say Never Again' was released on October 7th, 1983, and received largely positive reviews. It grossed $160 million at the box office.

Other Top 10 Films

'Trading Places' was next on the list of top 10 movies and starred Eddie Murphy, Dan Akroyd, Don Ameche, Jamie Lee Curtis, Ralph Bellamy, and Denholm Elliott. The film told the story of a poor street hustler (Murphy) and an upper-class broker (Aykroyd) and how they coped when their circumstances were swapped. It earned more than $90.4 million.

'Terms of Endearment', a drama/comedy family film, was adapted from a novel

Trading Places

of the same name written by Larry McMurtry in 1975. It had a great collection of movie stars, including Shirley MacLaine, Debra Winger, Danny DeVito, Jack Nicholson, John Lithgow, and Jeff Daniels. The story covered the relationship between MacLaine's character Aurora Greenway and Winger's character Emma, Aurora's daughter, spanning 30 years. It was initially released to a limited number of theaters on November 23rd, 1983, and then released more widely on December

Terms of Endearment

9th, 1983. It was a major success commercially, with a gross of over $108 million, and received eleven nominations at the Academy Awards, of which

Superman III

it won five awards, Best Picture, Best Director, Best Actress (MacLaine), Best Adapted Screenplay, and Best Supporting Actor (Nicholson).

The third installment of 'Superman,' 'Superman III,' wasn't as successful as the first two 'Superman' films, and with a budget of $39 million, it only grossed $80.2 million at the box office. It starred Christopher Reeve as Superman, Margot Kidder as Lois, Richard Pryor, Marc McClure, Pamela Stephenson, Jackie Cooper, and Annette O'Toole.

WarGames

'WarGames' also made it onto the top 10 movie list. This science fiction thriller starred Matthew Broderick, Ally Sheedy, Dabney Coleman, and John Wood. The plot was about a young hacker unintentionally accessing a military computer programmed to simulate, predict, and execute nuclear war. It was a success and received three Academy Award nominations. The film cost $12 million and grossed nearly $75 million worldwide.

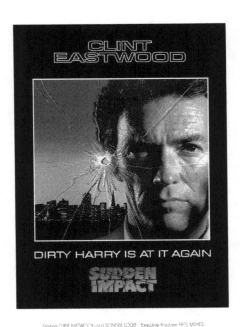

Sudden Impact

The Dirty Harry series continued in 1983, with the release of its fourth movie 'Sudden Impact,' starring Clint Eastwood. It was the only one of the Dirty Harry films that Eastwood directed himself. The film tells the story of a woman who is gang raped (played by Sondra Locke) and seeks revenge a decade later by killing each man. Perhaps the most famous movie phrase by Eastwood came from this movie, and "Go ahead, make my day" is still hugely popular today.

The last movie on the list of the top 10 was the legendary 'Staying Alive.' With a magical soundtrack by legends the Bee Gees and starring John Travolta, it carries on the story of Tony as he strives to have a professional dancing career. It was directed, co-written, and co-produced by none other than Sylvester Stallone and was one of only two films Stallone wrote but didn't star in, even though he makes a brief cameo appearance.

'Staying Alive' was released on July 15th, 1983, and received predominantly negative reviews. However, it was still a

Staying Alive

success at the Box Office with a gross of nearly $127 million worldwide and a budget of just $22 million. Interestingly, one of the songs from the movie 'Far from Over' was actually by Stallone's younger brother, Frank Stallone.

Top 1983 Movies at The Domestic Box Office (the-numbers.com)

Rank	Movie	Total Gross	Open Wknd. Gross
1	Star Wars Ep. VI: Return of the Jedi	$309,205,079	$23,019,618
2	Terms of Endearment	$108,423,489	$3,498,813
3	Flashdance	$90,463,574	$4,076,124
4	Trading Places	$90,400,000	$7,348,200
5	WarGames	$74,433,837	$6,227,804

Rank	Movie	Total Gross	Open Wknd. Gross
6	Octopussy	$67,900,000	$8,902,564
7	Sudden Impact	$67,642,693	$9,688,561
8	Mr. Mom	$64,800,000	$947,197
9	Staying Alive	$63,841,474	$12,146,143
10	Risky Business	$63,541,777	$4,275,327

Top 1983 Movies at The Worldwide Box Office (the-numbers.com)

Rank	Movie	Total Gross
1	Star Wars Ep. VI: Return of the Jedi	$475,106,177
2	Flashdance	$201,463,574
3	Octopussy	$187,500,000
4	Never Say Never Again	$160,000,000
5	Staying Alive	$126,041,474
6	Terms of Endearment	$108,423,749
7	Trading Places	$90,400,000
8	Superman III	$80,200,000
9	WarGames	$74,433,837
10	Sudden Impact	$67,642,69

Other Film Releases

There were so many great films released in 1983 and a few that became cult classics for decades to follow. One of these films was 'The Big Chill', with a star cast including Tom Berenger, Jeff Goldblum, William Hurt, Glenn Close, and Kevin Kline, just to name a few. The plot follows the reunion of a group of baby boomers 15 years after they left university when one of their

The Big Chill

Jaws 3-D

friends dies by suicide. The soundtrack was hugely popular.

Another popular movie was 'Jaws 3-D', the next in the chain of 'Jaws' movies. There had been increased interest and popularity in 3-D technology, which led to the film being produced in 3-D, but unfortunately, this limited the release because people at home couldn't see it in 3-D. It was still commercially successful, but the reviews were generally negative.

'Monty Python's The Meaning of Life,' with its stellar British cast, 'Cujo' by Stephen King about a rabid killer dog, and another cult classic, 'The Outsiders', with its cast of young 'brat packers' were also successful releases in 1983.

The Meaning of Life

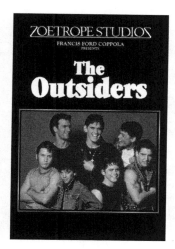

The Outsiders

40th Golden Globe Awards

The 40th Golden Globe Awards occurred on January 29th, 1983, at the Beverly Hilton Hotel, Beverly Hills, Los Angeles.

🏆 Winners

Best Picture Drama
E. T. The Extra-Terrestrial

Best Picture – Musical/Comedy
Tootsie

Best Actress – Motion Picture Drama
Meryl Streep (Sophie's Choice)

Best Actor – Motion Picture
Drama – Ben Kingsley (Gandhi)

Best Actress Motion Picture
Musical/Comedy
Julie Andrews (Victor Victoria)

Best Actor Motion Picture
Musical/Comedy
Dustin Hoffman (Tootsie)

Best Supporting Actress
Motion Picture
Jessica Lange (Tootsie)

Best Supporting Actor
Motion Picture Louis
Gossett Jr.
(An Officer and a
Gentleman)

Best Director Motion
Picture
Richard Attenborough
(Gandhi)

The 36th British Film Awards

The 36th British Film Awards occurred at Grosvenor House Hotel, London, on March 20th, 1983.

🏆 Winners

Best Actor in Film
Ben Kingsley (Gandhi)

Best Actress in Film
Katharine Hepburn (On Golden Pond)

Best Supporting Actor
Jack Nicholson (Reds)

Best Supporting Actress
Rohini Hattangadi (Gandhi)

Best Director Film
Richard Attenborough (Gandhi)

Best Film – Gandhi

Best Original Music – Pink Floyd
The Wall (Another Brick in The Wall)

The 55th Academy Awards

The ceremony for the 55th Academy Awards took place on April 11th, 1983, at the Dorothy Chandler Pavilion.

55th Academy Awards

🏆 Winners

- 🎖 Actor in a Leading Role – Ben Kingsley (Gandhi)

- 🎖 Actor in a Supporting Role – Louis Gossett Jr. (An Officer and a Gentleman)

- 🎖 Actress in a Leading Role – Meryl Streep (Sophie's Choice)

- 🎖 Actress in a Supporting Role – Jessica Lange (Tootsie)

- 🎖 Best Directing – Richard Attenborough (Gandhi)

- 🎖 Music (Original Score) – E.T. The Extra Terrestrial (John Williams)

- Music (Original Song) – 'Up Where We Belong', from An Officer and A Gentleman (music by Jack Nitzsche and Buffy Sainte-Marie, Lyrics by Will Jennings)

- Best Picture – Gandhi (Richard Attenborough, Producer)

Top of the Charts

Top Album – Police, Synchronicity

The top album for 1983 was 'Synchronicity' by the English band the Police. It was released on June 17th of the same year and included the hit singles 'Wrapped Around Your Finger,' 'Every Breath You Take,' 'Synchronicity, II' and 'King of Pain.'
At the Grammy Awards in 1984, 'Synchronicity' was nominated for five awards, winning three. At the

Synchronicity

time in Britain, they were considered the biggest band in the world due to their massive success. The album reached number one on the US Billboard 200 and the UK Albums Chart, and in the US alone, it sold more than 8 million copies. Rock magazine Rolling Stone listed the album in the '100 Best Albums of the Eighties' and the '500 Greatest Albums of All Time'. The album was inducted into the Grammy Hall of Fame in 2009.

Other Albums and Singles of 1983

There were a lot of notable single and album releases in 1983 that are still wildly popular today. These singles include 'Total Eclipse of the Heart' by Bonnie Tyler, 'We've Got Tonight' by Kenny Rogers and Sheena Easton,

Total Eclipse of the Heart

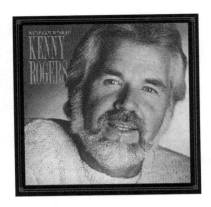

We've Got Tonight

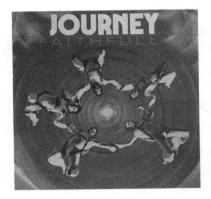

Faithfully

Tell Her About It

'Faithfully' by Journey, and 'Tell Her About It' by Billy Joel, just to name a few. For the most memorable albums of 1983 titles include 'Sweet Dreams (Are Made of This)' by the Eurythmics, 'Pyromania' by Def Leppard,

Sweet Dreams

Pyromania

'Eliminator' by ZZ Top, 'Flick of the Switch' by AC/DC, and 'Rebel Yell' by Billy Idol.

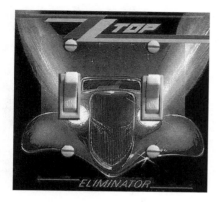

Eliminator

Flick of the Switch

Rebel Yell

Top Albums 1983 (tsort.info):

🏆 Winners

1. The Police – 'Synchronicity'
2. Lionel Richie – 'Can't Slow Down'
3. Original Soundtrack – 'Flashdance'
4. Culture Club – 'Colour by Numbers'
5. David Bowie – 'Let's Dance'
6. Pink Floyd – 'The Final Cut'

7. Billy Joel – 'An Innocent Man'
8. Genesis – 'Genesis'
9. U2 – 'War'
10. ZZ Top – 'Eliminator'

Top Singles 1983 (tsort.info):

🏆 **Winners**

1. Irene Cara – 'Flashdance... What a Feeling'
2. The Police – 'Every Breath You Take'
3. Michael Jackson – 'Billie Jean'
4. Culture Club – 'Karma Chameleon'
5. Michael Jackson – Beat It'
6. David Bowie – 'Let's Dance'
7. Bonnie Tyler – 'Total Eclipse of the Heart'
8. Lionel Richie – 'All Night Long (All Night)'
9. UB40 – 'Red Red Wine'
10. Paul McCartney/Michael Jackson – 'Say Say Say'

25th Annual Grammy Awards

Jeff Porcaro, Steve Porcaro, Mike Porcaro, David Paich, David Hungate, Bobby Kimball, and Steve Lukather in The 25th Annual Grammy Awards

The Awards were held at the Shrine Auditorium in Los Angeles on February 23rd, 1983, and were hosted by musician John Denver.

🏆 Winners

- Record of the Year – 'Rosanna' (Toto)

- Album of the Year – 'Toto IV' (Toto)

- Song of the Year – 'Always On My Mind' (Willie Nelson)

- Best New Artist – Men At Work

- Best Album of Original Score Written for A Motion Picture or A Television Special – 'E.T. The Extraterrestrial' (John Williams)

- Best Video – 'Physical' (Olivia Newton-John)

- Producer Of the Year (Non-Classical) – Toto

The 3rd Brit Awards

The 3rd Brit Awards took place at Grosvenor House Hotel in London on February 8th, 1983, hosted by Tim Rice.

Michael Jackson, Kim Wilde, Pete Townshend and Paul McCartney at the BRIT Awards

🏆 Winners

- 🎖 British Album of the Year – Barbara Streisand (Memories)
- 🎖 British Single of the Year – Dexys Midnight Runners (Come On Eileen)
- 🎖 British Female Solo Artist – Kim Wilde
- 🎖 British Male Solo Artist – Paul McCartney
- 🎖 British Group – Dire Straits
- 🎖 British Newcomer – Yazoo
- 🎖 British Producer of the Year – Trevor Horn
- 🎖 Outstanding Contribution to Music – The Beatles

Television

'The Winds of War' – Most Watched Miniseries in 1983

The Winds of War

The broadcast by ABC in America of 'The Winds of War' was the most watched miniseries of 1983, with a total of at least 140 million viewers. The miniseries was based on the book by the same name and included many significant events during World War II's first few years. Included in the show were actual documentary segments with narration by William Woodson, so the major events and certain characters could be explained.

January 23rd: The A-Team is Released on Television

'The A-Team' television series was based on former United States Army Special Forces Unit members. It was fictitious and was a massive hit throughout the 80s. The plot saw the team members being court-martialed for a crime they hadn't committed, and after they were sentenced to military prison, they escaped. From there, they worked as mercenaries, or soldiers of fortune, while they continued to try and clear their names and avoid being captured by the authorities.

The A-Team

Initially, the producers didn't think it would be that popular, but star George Peppard thought it would be massive before they even started filming. He was right. The show boosted the careers of its stars, especially Mr. T, who played the character B.A. Baracus. Mr. T became a global phenomenon, and some of his catchphrases were printed on shirts and other forms of merchandise. He even inspired a generation of mohawk haircuts.

In 2010 a feature film was produced by 20th Century Fox based on the series and starred none other than Bradley Cooper, who was hugely popular then.

February 28th: The Last Episode of M*A*S*H

The television series 'M*A*S*H' ran for eleven seasons, and on February 28th, 1983, the very last episode was broadcast. The episode, 'Goodbye, Farewell and Amen" was the most viewed television broadcast until the Super Bowl in February 2010. The final episode plot surrounds the last days of the Korean War at the 4077th M*A*S*H and examines the personal effect of the war on the characters. Because there was so much anticipation for the last episode, the CBS network broadcasting it increased the advertising cost to $450,000 per 30-second block. The original cast of 'M*A*S*H' included Alan Alda as surgeon Benjamin 'Hawkeye' Pierce and Wayne Rogers as surgeon 'Trapper' John McIntyre as the main protagonists. Larry Linville played the role of surgeon Frank Burns, and the head nurse Margaret 'Hot Lips' Houlihan, played by Loretta Swit. McLean Stevenson played Henry Blake, the company commander, and

M*A*S*H

Gary Burghoff was company clerk Walter 'Radar' O'Reilly, nicknamed 'Radar' because of his uncanny ability to hear helicopters from far away before anyone else could hear them. One of the most interesting characters was Maxwell Klinger, played by Jamie Farr, who spent all his time trying to get out of the Army, often dressing as a woman. The role of Father John Mulcahy, the Army chaplain, was played by William Christopher.

As time went on, some of the characters changed and were replaced. Wayne Rogers left and was replaced by Mike Farrell in the role of B.J. Hunnicutt. Harry Morgan's Sherman Potter replaced McLean Stevenson's Henry Blake. Frank Burns left, and David Ogden Stiers stepped in as surgeon Charles Emerson Winchester III.

Though there was a great deal of comedy in the series, there was the ever-present reminder of the cost of war, both physically and mentally. It depicted surgeons and nurses working amid horrible conditions with minimal supplies and the madness of some of the decisions made by the military. There was drama, grief, tragedy, and loss, sprinkled with humor, compassion, love, and a sense of mischief. It's no wonder why it was so massively popular and why the final episode was watched by so many.

December 2nd: Michael Jackson's Thriller Video Debuts

One of the greatest songs and music videos of all time, Michael Jackson's 14-minute video for 'Thriller', was broadcast for the first time. Since then, it has become the most often repeated music video of all time.

Because of the length of the video and the storyline, it is often referred to as a short film. It was groundbreaking for various reasons, including debuting in actual theaters and on television, and the production budget ended up costing double the initial $900,000 estimation.

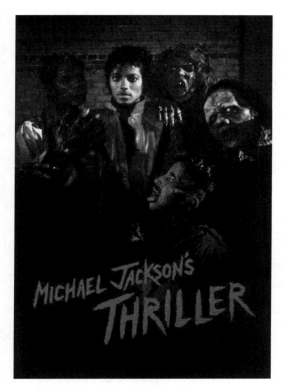

Michael Jackson's Thriller Music Video poster

As well as dancing zombies and some fantastic special effects makeup, the 'Thriller' video also included a voiceover by none other than Vincent Price, with his recognizable voice from the numerous horror movies he had made.

On YouTube, the music video has had over 790 million views, and the shorter version of the video has had over 100 million views. Years later, it is still popular on streaming platforms and currently has over 340 million plays.

📺 1982-83 Top Rated TV Shows (classic-tv.com)

Rank	Show	Estimated Audience
1	60 Minutes	21,241,500
2	Dallas	20,491,800
3	M*A*S*H	18,825,800
4	Magnum, P.I.	18,825,800
5	Dynasty	18,659,200
6	Three's Company	17,659,600
7	Simon & Simon	17,493,000
8	Falcon Crest	17,243,100
9	The Love Boat	16,909,900
10	The A-Team	16,743,300

📺 1983-84 Top Rated TV Shows (classic-tv.com)

Rank	Show	Estimated Audience
1	Dallas	21,536,600
2	60 Minutes	20,279,600
3	Dynasty	20,195,800
4	The A-Team	20,112,000
5	Simon & Simon	19,944,400
6	Magnum, P.I.	18,771,200
7	Falcon Crest	18,436,000

Rank	Show	Estimated Audience
8	Kate & Allie	18,352,200
9	Hotel	17,681,800
10	Cagney & Lacey	17,514,200

40th Golden Globe Awards

The 40th Golden Globe Awards took place at the Beverly Hilton Hotel in Los Angeles on January 29th, 1983. Hosted by John Forsythe and Julie Walters.

🏆 **Winners**

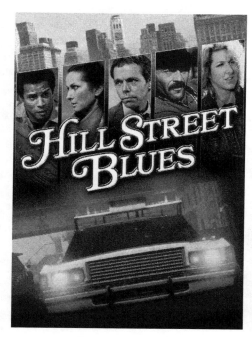

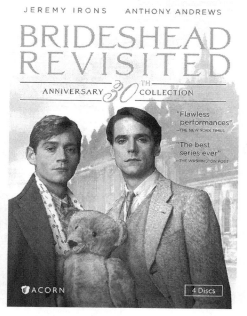

Best Drama Series
Hill Street Blues

Best Television Motion Picture
Brideshead Revisited

Best Musical/Comedy Series – Fame – TV Show

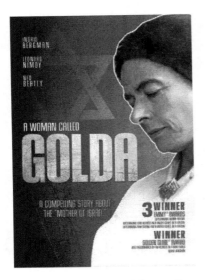

Best Actress – Television Motion Picture
Ingrid Bergman (A Woman Called Golda)

Best Actor – Television Motion Picture
Anthony Andrews (Brideshead Revisited)

Television Actress – Drama Series – Joan Collins, (Dynasty 1981-1989)

Best Television Actor – Drama Series
John Forsythe (Dynasty 1981-1989)

Best Television Actress – Musical/Comedy
Series – Debbie Allen (Fame – TV Show)

Best Television Actor – Musical/Comedy Series
Alan Alda (M*A*S*H -TV Show)

Best Supporting Actress – Television
Shelley Long (Cheers)

Best Supporting Actor – Television
Lionel Stander (Hart to Hart)

The 36th British Film Awards

The 36th British Film Awards took place at Grosvenor House Hotel in London on March 20th, 1983. Hosted by Frank Bough and Selina Scott.

🏆 Winners

Best Actor Television – Alec Guinness
(Smiley's People)

Best Television Actress – Beryl Reid
(Smiley's People)

Best Television Comedy Series
Yes, Minister (Peter Whitmore)

Best Television Drama Series or Serial
Boys from The Blackstuff
(Michael Wearing, Philip Saville)

Entertainment Performance – Nigel Hawthorne (Yes, Minister)

The 35th Primetime Emmy Awards

The 35th Primetime Emmy Awards were held at the Pasadena Civic Auditorium in California on September 25th, 1983. These awards were notable for the vulgar language, largely from Joan Rivers, who co-hosted with Eddie Murphy.

🏆 Winners

Outstanding Comedy Series
Cheers

Outstanding Lead Actor in A Comedy Series
Judd Hirsch

Outstanding Directing in
A Comedy Series
James Burrows (Cheers)

Outstanding Lead Actor in
A Drama Series
Ed Flanders (St. Elsewhere)

Outstanding Lead Actress in
A Drama Series
Tyne Daly (Cagney & Lacey)

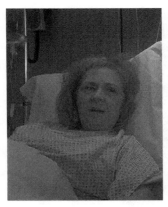

Outstanding Supporting
Actress in A Drama Series
Doris Roberts (St. Elsewhere)

Outstanding Supporting
Actor in A Drama Series
James Coco (St. Elsewhere)

Outstanding Supporting
Actor in a Comedy or Variety
or Music Series
Christopher Lloyd (Taxi)

Chapter IV: Sports Review 1983

American Sports

Super Bowl XVII

The Super Bowl XVII took place at the Rose Bowl in Pasadena, California, on January 30th, 1983. American Football Conference champion Miami Dolphins were up against the National Football Conference champion Washington

Super Bowl XVII logo

Redskins to determine the champion for the 1982 season.

The 1982 season had been shortened dramatically due to a player's strike, so teams only played nine regular season games, and a special 16-team, four-round playoff tournament was played that ignored the seeding in the divisions. The Washington Redskins had an NFC best 8-1 regular season record, and the Miami Dolphins finished at 7-2. With both through to the final, it became a rematch of the Super Bowl VII a decade before, where the Dolphins beat the Redskins.

In the second half of the game, the Redskins scored 17 points and

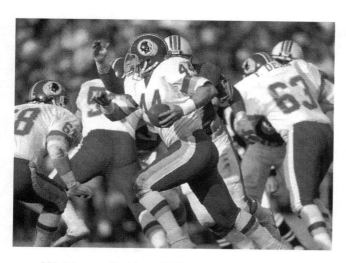

Washington Redskins Hall of Fame running back Riggins (44) runs upfield

gained a Super Bowl record of 276 yards while holding the Dolphins to 47 offensive plays and a total of 176 yards. However, by halftime, Miami was in the lead 17-10 with a 76-yard touchdown catch by Jimmy Cefalo and a 98-yard kickoff return by Fulton Walker. With just 10:10 remaining, the turning point came in the game. The Redskins were trailing the Dolphins 17-13, and with one yard to go at the 43-yard line of the Dolphins, Redskin running back John Riggins broke through the defense and scored a touchdown, putting the Redskins in the lead. Charlie Brown then scored an insurance touchdown. The Redskins defeated the Dolphins with the final score of 27-17, winning their first-ever Super Bowl championship. John Riggins was named MVP of the Super Bowl with two new Super Bowl records – most rushing yards of 166 and most rushing attempts (38) in a Super Bowl game.

Washington Redskins	Miami Dolphins
Alvin Garrett	Duriel Harris
Joe Jacoby	Jon Giesler
Russ Grimm	Bob Kuechenberg
Jeff Bostic	Dwight Stephenson
Fred Dean	Jeff Toews
George Starke	Eric Laakso
Don Warren	Bruce Hardy
Charlie Brown	Jimmy Cefalo
Joe Theismann	David Woodley
Rick Walker	Tony Nathan
John Riggins	Andra Franklin
Mat Mendenhall	Doug Betters

Washington Redskins	Miami Dolphins
Dave Butz	Bob Baumhower
Darryl Grant	Kim Bokamper
Dexter Manley	Bob Brudzinski
Mel Kaufman	A.J. Duhe
Neal Olkewicz	Earnie Rhone
Rich Milot	Larry Gordon
Jeris White	Gerald Small
Vernon Dean	Don McNeal
Tony Peters	Glenn Blackwood
Mark Murphy	Lyle Blackwood
Mark Moseley	Uwe von Schamann
Jeff Hayes	Tom Orosz

1983 Stanley Cup Finals

The National Hockey League's (NHL) Stanley Cup Finals for the 1982-83 season took place from May 10th – 17th, 1983. The contesting teams were the Campbell Conference champion Edmonton Oilers, who

1983 Stanley Cup Champion

were in the finals for the first time ever, and the defending Wales Conference and Cup champion, the New York Islanders, for who it was their fourth final appearance.

The Islanders won the Cup for the fourth consecutive year running and was the first time a North American professional sports team had won four titles consecutively in any league competition that comprised of more than 20 teams. The Stanley Cup of 1983 was the first one of eight consecutive Finals that were contested by an Alberta team. It was also the first time the Finals games had been played in Alberta. Following the competition, the Oilers were impressed by how the Islanders were in the locker room afterward, that they were more focused on tending to their injuries than celebrating. To the Oilers, this mindset taught them the level of dedication and sacrifice needed to be champions, and they would go on to win the Stanley Cup four times in the following five seasons. By 1990, they had won the Cup five times.

1983 NBA Finals

Julius Erving holds the Larry O'Brien Trophy

Often referred to as the 'Showdown '83', the NBA World Championship Series was the championship round of the NBA's 1982-83 season. The finals were between the Philadelphia 76ers and the Los Angeles Lakers. The series final was won by the Philadelphia 76ers, who beat the Lakers 4 games to 0. Center for the Philadelphia 76ers Moses Malone received the NBA Finals Most Valuable Player award.

This final in 1983, along with the final in 1989, were the only two times that they were not won by either the Boston

Celtics or the Los Angeles Lakers. Each Final throughout the decade featured either the Los Angeles Lakers or the Boston Celtics, and in 1984, 1985, and 1987, both teams faced off in the Finals.

Philadelphia 76ers	Los Angeles Lakers
Cheeks, Maurice	Abdul-Jabbar, Kareem
Cureton, Earl	Cooper, Michael
Edwards, Franklin	Johnson, Clay
Erving, Julius	Johnson, Magic
Iavaroni, Marc	Jones, Dwight
Johnson, Clemon	Jordan, Eddie
Johnson, Reggie	Landsberger, Mark
Jones, Bobby	McAdoo, Bob
Malone, Moses	McGee, Mike
McNamara, Mark	Mix, Steve
Richardson, Clint	Nixon, Norm
Toney, Andrew	Rambis, Kurt
	Wilkes, Jamaal
	Worthy, James

British Sports

1983 Five Nations Championship

The 54th series of the Five Nations Championship in rugby union took place in 1983, involving teams from France, Ireland, Wales, Scotland, and England.

Between January 21st and March 19th, 1983, ten rugby matches were played between the nations, and for the 17th time since the competition began, the winning spot was shared. At that point in time, there was no such thing as a tie-breaker, so France and Ireland shared the championship. It was the 5th time France had shared the title with another nation and the 8th time for Ireland. Patrick Estève, who played wing for France, earned the title of top try scorer, with a total of five tries against every other team in the tournament. The last time this was achieved was in 1925.

Patrick Estève playing for France against England

1983 FA Cup Final

Gordon Smith in action during the FA Cup final

The Cup was contested by teams Brighton & Hove Albion and Manchester United at Wembley Stadium. The favorites to win were Manchester United because Brighton & Hove Albion had come from the First Division that season and had not made it to a FA Cup Final previously. Manchester, on the other hand, had won the Cup four times before and had finished third that season in the league. The final match ended in a draw, with the teams scoring 2-2. This resulted in a replay being played five days later, and this time Manchester United won, with a final score of 4-0. For three years running, a replay had been necessary for the FA Cup Final due to draws.

1983 Wimbledon Championships

The infamous tennis championship competition took place between June 20th and July 3rd, 1983. It was played on a grass court at the All England Lawn Tennis and Croquet Club in Wimbledon, London. The 1983 championship was the 97th time it had been held. The winners were:

John McEnroe

- Men's Singles – John McEnroe, United States

- Women's Singles – Martina Navratilova, United States

- Men's Doubles – Peter Fleming/ John McEnroe, United States

- Women's Doubles – Martina Navratilova/Pam Shriver, United States

- Mixed Doubles – John Lloyd, United States, Wendy Turnbull, Australia

- Boys Singles – Stefan Edberg, Sweden

- Girls Singles – Pascale Paradis, France

- Boy's Doubles – Mark Kratzmann, Simon Youl, Australia

- Girl's Doubles – Patty Fendick, United States, Patricia Hy, Hong Kong

International Sports

Formula One World Championship 1983

The 37th season of
the FIA Formula One
World Championship
motor racing began
on March 13th
and concluded on
October 15th. This
competition included
a championship for
drivers and one for

Nelson Piquet in action during the F1 World Championship

constructors, which was competed for over 15 races.

The Driver's championship became a battle between Nelson Piquet (Brabham/ BMW), Alain Prost (Renault), René Arnoux (Ferrari) and Patrick Tambay (Ferrari). Prost had been leading the championship since the Belgian Grand Prix held in May until the last race in South Africa in October, but a problem with the turbo on his car forced him out. Nelson Piquet moved ahead and won the Driver's Championship for the second time. It was the first time the championship had been won by a turbocharged engine.

The Constructor's Championship title went to Ferrari, even though their top driver Arnoux only finished in third place. As well as the two championship titles being fought out on the track, there was a special non-championship race called the Race of Champions. World Champion Keke Rosberg, driving a Williams-Ford, took out the title.

The technical regulations had been changed for this season because of the number of serious and sometimes fatal accidents that had occurred during the racing season of 1982. Ground effect technology was banned, which resulted in the downforce and cornering speeds being reduced.

Chapter V: General 1983

Pop Culture

The Mario Bros. Debut

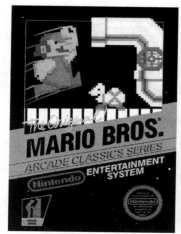 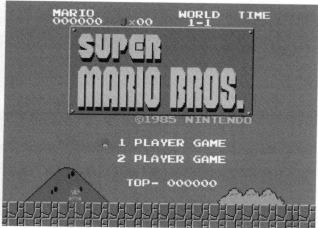

The Super Mario Bros. Game

The legendary Mario Bros. was first released in July 1983 in Japan, and it started out as an arcade game. The designer of the game was Shigeru Miyamoto, who also created the Legend of Zelda and Donkey Kong games. Another designer involved in the creation of Mario Bros. was Gunpei Yokoi, who also created Metroid and Game Boy.

The Mario Bros. game had a platform style and multiple phases, which made it exciting and interesting for younger players. The two main characters, Mario and Luigi, were Italian plumbers who had to fight creatures from the sewer. The concept of the Mario Bros. was based in New York.

You might be surprised to learn that initially, Mario Bros. was not all that popular. At the time it was released, the video game industry was undergoing a crash, so fewer people were playing the games. But, when it was re-released in 1985 as the Super Mario Bros, it became the legendary massive hit that it still is today.

Swatches

1983 Swatch Collection

If you were living in the 80s, one of the biggest fashion trends was the Swatches. In 1983 Swiss watch manufacturers came out with the Swatch, which were brightly colored plastic watches that were inexpensive and comfortable to wear. The name 'Swatch' stood for 'second watch,' which suggested the watches were quite disposable and didn't cost a fortune to purchase.

The Swatches were really popular with the younger generations, largely due to the amazing array of colors available, and because they were so cheap, some people would own several at a time so they could coordinate with their clothing each day. Some even wore multiple Swatches at a time!

Ray-Ban Sunglasses

Despite being around for quite some time, in 1983, Ray-Bans really became a fashion item. This is largely due to movie star Tom Cruise, who wore the Ray-Ban Wayfarers in the movie 'Risky Business.' Later he wore the Aviator

Tom Cruise wearing ray-ban

style of Ray-Bans in the movie 'Top Gun,' which really propelled Ray-Bans to the top of the fashion list. Thanks to the release of these two movies, the sunglasses experienced large increases in sales.

The Moonwalk

If you were a kid in the 80s, you knew about the Moonwalk and spent hours trying to learn how to do it. The man behind this famous dance move was none other than Michael Jackson. On March 25th, 1983, a special was played on television called Motown 25: Yesterday, Today, Forever, to celebrate the 25th anniversary of Motown, a record label that came under the Universal Music Group. Michael Jackson performed his hit 'Billie Jean' for the special, and he did the Moonwalk for the very first time in public. From then on, the Moonwalk would become part of Michael Jackson's legacy, and

Michael Jackson performs 'Billie Jean' on the TV show Motown 25

for many people, it is hard to think of one without automatically thinking of the other. It was his signature step.

Madonna's Influence on Fashion

When Madonna hit the television screens in 1983, she had a major influence on fashion, particularly on females. She was often dressed in crop tops, short skirts or mesh shorts, lace gloves, and large headbands that were like ribbons. She would often shock the audience on red carpets with her unique style, and some of her fashion choices became just as famous as the singer herself. Her music videos and concerts had a massive effect on young women and their wardrobes in particular.

Madonna

Fraggle Rock Debut

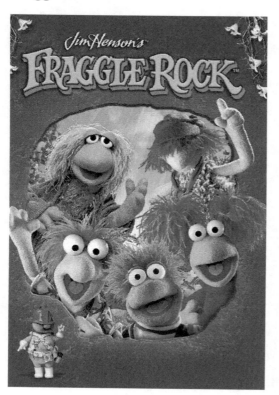

Fraggle Rock

Jim Henson, the man behind the creation of the Muppets, created and produced a television show called 'Fraggle Rock' in January 1983. It was produced to be available in other countries in different languages so it could reach a much wider audience. Although it was aimed at children, the fantasy creatures called Fraggles, Doozers, and Gorgs were used to tackle more serious issues like personal identity, prejudice, environment, social conflict, and spirituality.

McNuggets Are Born

McNuggets Ad Flyer

McDonald's introduced an item to their menu that would become a global phenomenon in the shape of small bite-size pieces of battered chicken. The McNuggets were so popular they stayed on the menu and are still there today.

Technological Advancements

Motorola Introduces Mobile Phones

In 1983, the Motorola Company released the first mobile phone that was available to the public. The phone was called the DynaTAC, and it cost around $4,000 to purchase! It was also a heavy and bulky brick of a phone compared to the phones we have now. It was mainly the wealthy members of the public that were able to afford the phones at first, but everyone wanted one!

Motorola DynaTAC 8000X

The Internet

The official birthday of the internet is considered to be January 1st, 1983. Before then, computer networks did not have a way to communicate with each other. The establishment of a new communications protocol was called the Transfer Control Protocol/Internetwork Protocol (TCP/IP). This protocol enabled computers on different networks to basically talk to one another. ARPANET and the Defense Data Network changed to the TCP/IP standard officially on January 1st, which was ultimately the birth of the internet. Now all the different networks could be connected by a language that was universal.

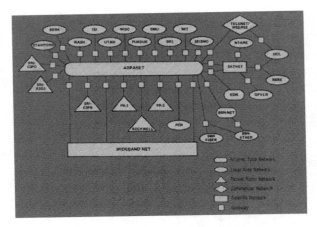

Internet Topographic Map, 1983

Microsoft Word is Launched

On October 25th, 1983, Microsoft Corporation launched Multi-Tool Word, which would soon become known as Microsoft Word. Initially, it could only be used on computers that ran a form of UNIX system but later that year, they rewrote the program so it could be used on personal computers under the DOS system, which is when the name was changed to Microsoft Word. At the time, there had been two other similar products released the year before, called WordStar and WordPerfect, and Microsoft Word was in direct competition with them

Microsoft Word 1.0

Just like the program Word Star, Word is what they called WYSIWYG, which stands for 'what you see is what you get,' meaning that how you saw the document on the screen was exactly how it would print out. When Word came out, it was the first program where the computer mouse was used extensively. It also had font styles such as bold, italic, and underlining and had the ability to use multiple windows at a time. By 1985, the versions included spell check and word count, along with a number of other features. Microsoft Word is perhaps the most used program globally today.

Pioneer 10 Passes the Orbit of Neptune

NASA's Pioneer 10, a space probe that was launched in 1972 and weighed just 260kg or 570 pounds, was the first mission to the outer planets, and it was a remarkable success, with a series of firsts accomplished.

Artist Depiction of Pioneer 10 that passed beyond Neptune's orbit

On June 13th, 1983, Pioneer 10 crossed the orbit of Neptune, which was the most outer planet from the sun at the time. This was the very first time an object made by man had been able to go beyond the furthest away planet.

First CD Players Released in America

First CD Player

Compact discs were first launched in Japan, but they didn't appear in America until March 1983. You could only purchase CDs in 75 stores across the State, and you had to be willing to pay a considerable amount of money to own them. A Sony or Magnavox CD player would set you back around $900, and the disks ranged between $16 and $20 each.

In 1983, 35,000 CD players were sold in America. In comparison, there were 236.8 million tapes and 209.6 million LPs sold compared to just 770,000 CDs.

The very first CD made in America was Bruce Springsteen's 'Born in the USA' album in 1984. That year, it is estimated that 16.4 million CDs were sold worldwide.

Last Hand-Cranked Telephones in the US Taken Out of Service

Hand-Cranked Telephone

The last remaining hand-cranked telephones were finally taken out of service in 1983 in the United States. The town of Bryant Pond, Maine, had still been using them, and on the day they were scheduled to be switched over, the locals were invited to gather at the home of Elden Hathaway, who had operated the telephone Co. from his home between 1952 – 1981, so they could watch the last call being made to the switchboard.

With just a flick of a switch, the 425 telephone subscribers joined the dial-it-yourself modern world. Many people weren't that keen, especially those who worked on the switchboard. All of the old phone equipment, including a cradle phone and an oak box with a crank handle, was sold to subscribers for just $3 each. The rest of the stock was auctioned.

Fashion

80s Glam Rock Era

Everything about fashion in 1983 was big, from the big hair to the big shoulder pads to the big, bold makeup. It was the glam rock era, with loads of hairspray and heavy black eyeliner. But other fashion trends defined 1983 as well. It was a time women wanted to look like men, and men wanted to look like women.

Colors were typically bright, with neon featuring prominently, including the workout leotards and leg warmers as Jazzercise and other forms of exercise became popular. Women also learned the art of power dressing, with well-cut blazers and skirts, and collars were always turned up.

Vogue, March 1983

Heather Locklear poses for a fashion portrait shoot

A major fashion accessory in 1983 was the big belt. Again, everything had to be big! The waist was cinched and accentuated, and the belts were used with pants, skirts, and coats. Combined with the huge shoulder pads found in tops and jackets, the belt helped create a feminine shape.

A typical outfit might consist of a skirt and leggings, an oversized shirt with shoulder

Vogue, 1983   Vogue UK, 1983

pads cinched at the waist by a large, sometimes ornate belt. It was common for girls and women to wear the Rah-Rah skirt with 3/4 length leggings underneath, often in contrasting colors or patterns. Speaking of patterns, bold art-like patterns were popular, as were stripes. Or the skirt and leggings could be switched out with a pair of designer jeans that were all the rage at the time.

The most popular jeans in 1983 were made by Guess, with their signature triangle sewn onto the back pocket. At that time, stonewashed denim was starting to make its way into wardrobes worldwide and would continue to be popular throughout the next few decades.

Stonewashed denim

Fashion for men in 1983 ran the gamut of styles, from the full glam to the Hawaiian shirts made famous by Tom Selleck in 'Magnum P.I.'. Many young men wore pastel-colored polo shirts with collars turned up. Men were also fans of oversized coats and large belts, and yes, they also were fond of shoulder pads, just like the women!

Tom Selleck as Thomas Magnum

For girls and women, the most popular shoe of 1983 was the Jelly Shoe. Crafted initially from fisherman's PVC plastic shoes, the Jelly Shoe came in various colors in footwear that hadn't been seen before. Sometimes there was glitter infused into the plastic. They grew in popularity when the owners of Jelly Shoes entered a partnership with an exporter in Grendene in 1982. The following year, the sales of the shoes multiplied by 20.

Jelly Shoes

They were everywhere, and before you knew it, some of the most famous designers, such as Jean-Paul Gaultier and Thierry Mugler, were designing them.

Cars

Car Sales By Company (nytimes.com)

For the model year ending on September 30th, 1983, ten of the best-selling cars belonged to General Motors. But Ford's Escort was one of the best-selling cars, with more than 250,000 of that model being sold.

The second most-sold car was the Cutlass from General Motors, then the Chevrolet, the Oldsmobile 88, the Cavalier, Chevette, Camaro, and the Ciera.

🚗 Sales Figures

1. General Motors – 3,876,006 units
2. Ford – 1,481,382 units
3. Chrysler – 819,209 units
4. A.M.C. – 183,005 units
5. Volkswagen of America Inc. – 83,222 units
6. Honda of America – 24,073 units

🚗 Most Popular Cars 1983

1983 Oldsmobile Cutlass Supreme

Although it was beaten in 1982 sales numbers by the Ford Escort, the Oldsmobile was still the most popular vehicle in 1983. Sales reached a record high when the Cutlass Ciera was released. The Cutlass was a mid-sized personal luxury coupe with an automatic 3-speed gearbox, a

Oldsmobile Cutlass Supreme

top speed of 101mph (163kph), and RWD. It wasn't considered a muscle car but had the speed and power to be considered among the best of them.

1983 Pontiac 6000STE

Pontiac 6000STE

The A-bodies produced by General Motors had been the best since 1977, and top of the list was the Pontiac 6000STE. This car contained the most up-to-date technology from General Motors and was wrapped in sheet metal, which was considered controversial at the time. Its appearance was distinctive, it was economical and fun to drive, and one of the most comfortable vehicles of the time.

1983 Toyota Celica Supra

The Toyota Celica Supra was one of the most popular cars in 1983 for a number of reasons. It wasn't a big car, but it had a big engine, with six cylinders which created a beautiful smooth sound when they were running. The Celica

Toyota Celica Supra

Supra had fuel injection to add to its power. The interior was considered state-of-the-art and the bodywork distinctive, and it was known to have one of the best sound systems available. It was unlike the traditional American cars, and eventually, this is what made it a great selling point. It was lighter, smaller, and had plenty of grunt under the hood.

Popular Recreation

Atari 5200 Gaming System

By 1983, video arcades weren't as popular as a hang-out for kids because their home systems were becoming more common, so they stayed home and played instead. The Atari 5200 Gaming System was released in 1982 but became the main home gaming system in 1983. However, the most popular arcade games included Star Wars, Donkey Kong 3, Mario Bros., and Dragon's Lair. Other popular video games included 3-Demon, Alpha Blaster, Bonka, Baseball, 3D Crazy Coaster, MotoRace USA, Space Cowboy, Chariot Race, and Pac & Pal.

One of the most popular toys in 1983 was the G.I Joe Swivel Arm Battle Grip. This version of the G.I. Joe action figure had arms that could swivel, enabling them to hold onto their weapons and accessories better than before.

Perhaps the most sensational toy of 1983 was the Cabbage Patch Kids. Initially developed in 1978, it wasn't until the 1980s that these one-of-a-kind hand-stitched dolls really took off globally. At first, they were called 'The Little People' dolls, but the name

G.I Joe toy with Swivel Arm Battle Grip

Cabbage Patch Kids

Hasbro Glo Worm

changed to Cabbage Patch Kids in 1982. Each doll wasn't 'sold' but instead adopted, and they had their own names and birth certificates.

Another toy that was a huge success and is still available today is the Hasbro Glo Worm. It is a plush soft toy with a battery device that makes the head of the toy light up when the body is squeezed. Many babies and toddlers had Glo Worms, and because it was so successful, Hasbro created a line of night lights, videos, storybooks, and other types of merchandise.

The Smurfs

Cartoons were popular on Saturday mornings in 1983, including The Smurfs, Bugs Bunny, Spider-Man, Flintstones, Scooby and Scrappy Doo, and Shirt Tales. Although it didn't air on Saturday mornings, another super popular cartoon was He-Man and the Masters of the Universe, which first aired on television in September 1983. The show had a large following, and the toys that were created from the series are collectible today.

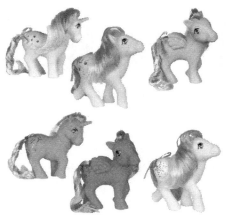

My Little Pony Classic Rainbow Ponies

Care Bears Plush

Other popular toys from 1983 that were on many Christmas wish lists were the Care Bears and My Little Pony toys. The Care Bears started as paintings for greeting cards but were turned into soft multi-colored teddy bears in 1983. From there, they were developed into a television series and three movies. Each bear has a unique picture on its tummy to represent its personality. The bears later had a revival in 2002 and 2012 and are still very popular today.

Chapter VI: Births & Deaths 1983

Births (onthisday.com)

February 7th – Alexander Dreymon: German Actor

February 10th – Vic Fuentes: American Singer, Songwriter, and Musician

February 23rd – Emily Blunt: British Actress

March 1st – Lupita Nyong'o: Kenyan-Mexican Actress

March 10th – Carrie Underwood: American Country Singer

March 23rd – Mo Farah: British Long-Distance Runner

May 5th – Henry Cavill: British Actor

May 26th – Scott Disick: American Media Personality and Socialite

May 28th – Roman Atwood: American YouTuber and Prankster

June 19th – Macklemore: American Rapper

June 30th – Cheryl Ann Tweedy: English Singer and Television Personality

August 11th – Chris Hemsworth: Australian Actor

August 14th – Mila Kunis: American Actress

August 20th – Andrew Garfield: English and American Actor

September 14th – Amy Winehouse: English Singer and Songwriter

September 25th – Donald Glover: American Actor, Rapper, Singer, Writer and Comedian

October 2nd – Huda Kattan: American Makeup Artist, Beauty Blogger, and Entrepreneur

October 21st – Amber Rose: American Model and Television Personality

November 7th – Adam Devine: American Actor, Comedian, Singer, Screenwriter, and Producer

November 10th – Miranda Lambert: American Country Music Singer and Songwriter

November 19th – Adam Driver: American Actor

November 20th – Future: American Rapper

November 21st -Nikki Bella: American Professional Wrestler and Television Personality

November 21st – Brie Bella: American Professional Wrestler and Television Personality

November 28th – Summer Rae: American Professional Wrestler, Model, Actress, Ring Announcer

December 2nd – Aaron Rodgers: American Football Player

December 20th – Jonah Hill: American Actor, Comedian, and Filmmaker

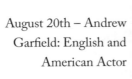

Deaths (onthisday.com)

January 9th – Stan Spence: American Major League Baseball Center Fielder

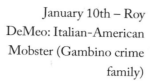
January 10th – Roy DeMeo: Italian-American Mobster (Gambino crime family)

January 11th – Nikolai V. Podgorny: President of the USSR

January 15th – Meyer Lansky: Polish-born American Mobster known as the "Mob's Accountant"

January 24th – George Cukor: American Film Director and Film Producer

January 28th – Billy Fury: English Singer, Musician, Songwriter, and Actor

February 4th – Karen Carpenter: American Singer and Drummer

February 25th – Tennessee Williams: American Playwright and Screenwriter

April 4th – Gloria Swanson: American Actress and Producer

April 14th – Pete Farndon: English Bassist

April 23rd – Clarence "Buster" Crabbe: American Olympic Swimmer and Actor

April 30th – George Balanchine: Georgian-American Ballet Choreographer

April 30th – Muddy Waters: American Blues Singer and Musician

May 31st – Jack Dempsey: American Boxer

June 30th – Bo Gentry: American Pop Singer, Songwriter and Record Producer

July 29th – David Niven: British Soldier, Actor, Memoirist, and Novelist

August 17th – Ira Gershwin: American Lyricist

October 10th – Sir Ralph Richardson: British Actor

October 31st – George Halas (Papa Bear): American NFL Coach and Owner of the Chicago Bears

November 22nd – Michael Conrad: American Actor

December 8th – Slim Pickens: American Rodeo Performer and Actor

December 8th – Keith Holyoake: 26th Prime Minister of New Zealand

December 28th - Jimmy Demaret: American Golfer

December 28th - Dennis Wilson: American Musician, Singer, and Songwriter who Co-founded the Beach Boys

Chapter VII: Statistics 1983

* U.S. GDP 1983 – 3.634 trillion USD (worldbank.org)

* U.S. GDP 2021- 23.00 trillion USD (tradingeconomics.com)

* U.K. GDP 1983 – 489.6 billion USD (worldbank.org)

* U.K. GDP 2021 -3186.86 billion USD (tradingeconomics.com)

* U.S. Inflation (% Change in C.P.I.) 1983 – 3.2% (worldbank.org)

* U.S. Inflation (% Change in C.P.I.) 2021 – 4.7% (worldbank.org)

* U.K. Inflation (% Change in C.P.I.) 1983 -4.6% (worldbank.org)

* U.K. Inflation (% Change in C.P.I.) 2021 – 2.5% (worldbank.org)

* U.S. Population 1983 – 233.8 million (worldbank.org)

* U.S. Population 2021 – 331,893.74 (worldbank.org)

* U.K. Population 1983 – 56.33 million (worldbank.org)

* U.K. Population 2021 – 67,326.57 (worldbank.org)

* U.S. Population by Gender 1983 -F: 119,129,099M: 114,662,901 (worldbank.org)

* U.S. Population by Gender 2021 -F: 167,669,677M: 164,224,068 (worldbank.org)

* U.K. Population by Gender 1983 -F: 28,937,670 M: 27,395,178 (worldbank.org)

* U.K. Population by Gender 2021- F: 34,045,551M: 33,281,018 (worldbank.org)

* U.S. Life Expectancy at Birth 1983 – 74 (worldbank.org)

* U.S. Life Expectancy at Birth 2020 - 77 (worldbank.org)

* U.K. Life Expectancy at Birth 1983 – 74 (worldbank.org)

* U.K. Life Expectancy at Birth 2020 – 81 (worldbank.org)

* U.S. Annual Working Hours Per Worker 1983 – 1779h (ourworldindata.org)

* U.S. Annual Working Hours Per Worker 2017 – 1757h (ourworldindata.org)

* U.K. Annual Working Hours Per Worker 1983 – 1740h (ourworldindata.org)

* U.K. Annual Working Hours Per Worker 2017 –1670h (ourworldindata.org)

* U.S. Unemployment Rate 1983 – 9.6 (index.mundi.com)

* U.S. Unemployment Rate 2019 – 3.788 (index.mundi.com)

* U.K. Unemployment Rate 1983 -11.475 (index.mundi.com)

* U.K. Unemployment Rate 2019 – 4.229 (index.mundi.com)

* U.S. Total Tax Revenue 1983 – 24.01% (ourworldindata.org)

* U.S. Total Tax Revenue 2020 – 25.02% (ourworldindata.org)

* U.K. Total Tax Revenue 1983 – 32.29% (ourworldindata.org)

* U.K. Total Tax Revenue 2020 – 34.26% (ourworldindata.org)

* U.S. Prison Population 1980- 503,586 (prisonstudies.org)

* U.S. Prison Population 2018 – 2,102,400 (prisonstudies.org)

* U.K. Prison Population 1980 – 43,109 (prisonstudies.org)

* U.K. Prison Population 2020 – 79,514 (prisonstudies.org)

* U.S. Cost of Living: $100 in 1983 would equate to the spending power of $ 297.50 in 2022. That is a total change of 197.50% in 39 years (in2013dollars.com).

* U.K. Cost of Living: £100 in 1983 would equate to the spending power of £ £375.07 in 2022. That is a total change of 275.07% in 39 years (in2013dollars.com).

Cost of Things

United States

* One Dozen Eggs – $0.89 (stacker.com)

* One Pound of White Bread – $0.54 (stacker.com)

* Half-Gallon of Fresh Milk – $1.13 (stacker.com)

* Average Salary Per Person – $15,239.24 (wikipedia.org)

* Average Cost of a House – $75,300 (gobankingrates.com)

* Average Price of a Car – $ 9,175 (cheapism.com)

* Average Price of a Gallon of Petrol – $1.16 (titlemax.com)

United Kingdom

* One Dozen Eggs – £0.66 (ons.gov.uk)

* Loaf Of White Bread – £0.38 (ons.gov.uk)

* Pint Of Milk – £0.21 (ons.gov.uk)

* Average Salary Per Person – £5,876 (thisismoney.co.uk)

* ⭐ Average Cost of a House – £27,3623 (loveproperty.com)

* ⭐ Price of a Car (Ford Escort RS1600i)- £6,700 (motoringresearch. com)

* ⭐ Average Price of a Gallon of Petrol – £1.67 (speedlimit.org.uk)

Chapter VIII: Iconic Advertisements of 1983

Mercury Grand Marquis

Beefeater Gin

Virginia Slims

Tide

Quaker Halfsies

Ford Telstar

Fila

Jim Beam Bourbon Whiskey

Kodak: Kodamatic Trimprint Instant
Color Film

Sprite: Sugar Free

Pontiac: 1983 Bonneville

Adidas

Burger King & Pepsi:
a young Sarah Michelle Gellar

Martini & Rossi

The IBM Personal Computer

Camel Lights

Jeep Wagoneer

Sony Sports Walkman

Smirnoff: with Robert Ludlum

Campbell's Soup

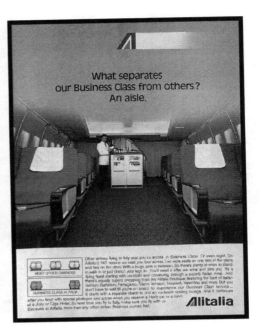

Alitalia Airline

Redex

Coca-Cola

Nike

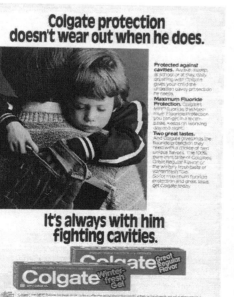

Listerine

Colgate

Budweiser

Dickies Coveralls

Jose Cuervo Tequila

Marlboro

I have a gift for you!

Dear reader, thank you so much for reading my book!

To make this book more (much more!) affordable, the images are all black & white, but I've created a special gift for you!

You can now have access, for FREE, to the PDF version of this book with the original images!

Keep in mind that some are originally black & white, but a lot of them are colored.

I hope you enjoy it!

Download it here:

https://bit.ly/3uDHjqy

Or Scan this QR Code:

I have a favor to ask you!

I deeply hope you've enjoyed reading this book and felt transported right into 1983!

I loved researching it, organizing it, and writing it, knowing that it would make your day a little brighter.

If you've enjoyed it too, I would be extremely grateful if you took just a few minutes to leave a positive customer review and share it with your friends.

As an unknown author, that makes all the difference and gives me the extra energy I need to keep researching, writing, and bringing joy to all my readers. Thank you!

Best regards,
Michael B. Allen

Please leave a positive book review here:

https://bit.ly/3iDb203

Or Scan this QR Code:

Check Our Other Books!

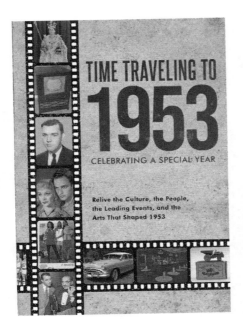